FEARLESS
CONVERSATION™

WHY IS JESUS SO RADICAL?

DISCUSSIONS FROM MATTHEW AND LUKE

PARTICIPANT GUIDE

Loveland, CO

Group
Real. **Bold.** Love.

Group resources really work!

This Group resource incorporates our R.E.A.L. approach to ministry. It reinforces a growing friendship with Jesus, encourages long-term learning, and results in life transformation, because it's:

Relational—Learner-to-learner interaction enhances learning and builds Christian friendships.

Experiential—What learners experience through discussion and action sticks with them up to 9 times longer than what they simply hear or read.

Applicable—The aim of Christian education is to equip learners to be both hearers and doers of God's Word.

Learner-based—Learners understand and retain more when the learning process takes into consideration how they learn best.

Fearless Conversation: Why Is Jesus So Radical?
Discussions from Matthew and Luke
Participant Guide

Copyright © 2014 Group Publishing, Inc.

Visit our website: **group.com**

Fearless Conversation adult Sunday school curriculum is created by the amazing adult ministry team at Group. Contributing writers for this quarter are:

Susan Lawrence
Larry Shallenberger
Doug Schmidt
Thomas Smith

ISBN 978-1-4707-1350-8

Printed in the United States of America.

10 9 8 7 6 5 4 3 2 1   21 20 19 18 17 16 15 14

CONTENTS

HERE'S WHAT A LESSON LOOKS LIKE

Your leader will guide each lesson through four sections:

GREETING

Make new friends and start the conversation as the topic for the week is introduced.

GROUNDING

This is where you read the Scripture for the week. The Bible content is always provided here in the participant guide. After hearing God's Word read aloud, you'll have the opportunity to follow the inductive study method of writing down first responses, questions, thoughts, or ideas that are sparked by the Bible reading.

GRAPPLING

Here's where the conversation deepens. You'll find questions that are intentionally challenging to answer. These won't have easy answers and you won't have a fill-in-the-blank option. Everyone will wrestle with the questions that the lesson provides, as well as their own questions that they're wondering about. The leader will ask God to guide the conversation—and you can join in that prayer! Remember to treat others with respect during these conversations, even if you don't agree with them. Listen first. Speak second.

GROWING

Here's where the personal application comes in. You'll have the chance to reflect on what God's Word, as shared in this lesson, means to you for your own life and determine what your personal response is.

Throughout each lesson you'll also find two other helps:

BEHIND THE SCENES

These sections of commentary and notes from Bible scholars will give you additional context into history, language, culture, and other relevant information. You can read these sections ahead of time or during the lesson—whichever works best for you.

GOING DEEPER

These tips will help you be a great conversationalist. They remind you how to keep a conversation going, how to be a better listener, and how to be respectful even if you don't agree with someone.

FINAL TIP:

Have a sense of divine anticipation. Approach each class with a heart full of anticipation over what God might do that day. God is alive and present with you and your class. Always prepare by praying, asking God to help you see his hand at work in the conversation. Trust God to show up and show you and others in the class exactly where he wants the conversation to go!

EARLESS ONVERSATION™

WHY IS JESUS SO RADICAL?

LESSON 1:
WHY DID GOD COME AS A BABY?

GREETING

BEHIND THE SCENES

Luke 2:1-20 describes Joseph and Mary's journey to Bethlehem and the birth of Jesus. Certainly it had been difficult for them to endure the stares and overhear the snickers of acquaintances who noticed that Mary had become pregnant prior to the completion of their marriage. Now she and Joseph were forced by the Romans to travel from their home in Nazareth to his ancestral home of Bethlehem. This was a journey of about 70 miles. Although popular renditions of this trip usually show Mary riding a donkey, she and Joseph probably weren't wealthy enough to own one. It's more likely that they had to walk all the way, even though Mary was close to her time to deliver. ▼

> You'll find "Behind the Scenes" boxes with Bible commentary provided throughout this lesson. You can read these ahead of time or as you move through the lesson. They're there to help you gain a better understanding of the Bible.

The exact date of Jesus' birth is impossible to calculate. According to Luke 2:2, the census occurred when Quirinius was governor of Syria. His first term occurred from 6 to 4 B.C., so Jesus was likely born between those dates. Unfortunately, the date of Jesus' birth was miscalculated when the Christian calendar was created hundreds of years later.

**Why does it matter where we are born?
Or…does it matter at all?**

Our message to the goldfish:

How we will deliver this message:

**How do you think this activity of communicating
to a goldfish relates to God communicating with us?**

GROUNDING

God's Word: Luke 2:1-20

[1] In those days Caesar Augustus issued a decree that a census should be taken of the entire Roman world. [2] (This was the first census that took place while Quirinius was governor of Syria.) [3] And everyone went to their own town to register.

[4] So Joseph also went up from the town of Nazareth in Galilee to Judea, to Bethlehem the town of David, because he belonged to the house and line of David. [5] He went there to register with Mary, who was pledged to be married to him and was expecting a child. [6] While they were there, the time came for the baby to be born, [7] and she gave birth to her firstborn, a son. She wrapped him in cloths and placed him in a manger, because there was no guest room available for them.

[8] And there were shepherds living out in the fields nearby, keeping watch over their flocks at night. [9] An angel of the Lord appeared to them, and the glory of the Lord shone around them, and they were terrified. [10] But the angel said to them, "Do not be afraid. I bring you good news that will cause great joy for all the people. [11] Today in the town of David a Savior has been born to you; he is the Messiah, the Lord. [12] This will be a sign to you: You will find a baby wrapped in cloths and lying in a manger."

[13] Suddenly a great company of the heavenly host appeared with the angel, praising God and saying, [14] "Glory to God in the highest heaven, and on earth peace to those on whom his favor rests."

▼

[15] When the angels had left them and gone into heaven, the shepherds said to one another, "Let's go to Bethlehem and see this thing that has happened, which the Lord has told us about."

[16] So they hurried off and found Mary and Joseph, and the baby, who was lying in the manger. [17] When they had seen him, they spread the word concerning what had been told them about this child, [18] and all who heard it were amazed at what the shepherds said to them. [19] But Mary treasured up all these things and pondered them in her heart. [20] The shepherds returned, glorifying and praising God for all the things they had heard and seen, which were just as they had been told.

What are the first questions that come to mind? What sort of jumps out at you and catches your attention? Capture those thoughts here.

GRAPPLING

GOING DEEPER

You can help others in your group go deeper by listening with your full attention and by asking questions as others share. Saying "I wonder about what you just said. Tell me more!" will help people know you care about what they're saying and want them to open up more.

From this account in Luke 2, what do you learn about the nature of God?

What is God communicating to us by coming as a baby? And what do you think motivated God to do this?

INTERESTING THOUGHTS SPARKED
BY OTHERS IN MY GROUP:

BEHIND THE SCENES

It's significant that Jesus' birth was announced first to shepherds for several reasons. First, this is a reminder that Jesus was from the line of David, who was a shepherd. Second, in those days shepherds were not highly thought of. They were considered so unreliable that their testimony was not accepted in the courts, and they were deemed unclean by the orthodox religious establishment. The fact that Jesus' birth was announced first to them indicates that Jesus came to earth for everyone, both "clean" and "unclean." It also foreshadows the common people's acceptance of Christ and the religious leadership's rejection of him. Finally, Jesus described himself as the good shepherd. Love and care were central to his time on earth.

What other reasons can you think of?

What is the significance of the manger?

GROWING

Luke 2:17-20 tells us how different people responded to the birth of Jesus. The shepherds told others about what they'd seen and heard, and they praised God. The people who heard what the shepherds said were amazed. Mary "treasured up all these things and pondered them in her heart."

What about you? God came to earth as a baby, placed in a manger, for you. What does this mean to you? How do you respond?

Write your reflections here.

PARTICIPANT GUIDE

As we move through this quarter, we'll continually be wondering on the question, Why is Jesus so radical? Based only on what we've discussed today, what's one sentence that might answer that question?

Write your thoughts here.

FEARLESS
CONVERSATION™

WHY IS
JESUS SO
RADICAL?

P A R T I C I P A N T   G U I D E

LESSON 2: CAN WE REALLY BEAT TEMPTATION?

GREETING

BEHIND THE SCENES

Satan in Hebrew means "adversary" or "accuser." Matthew 4:1-11 describes Jesus' interactions with Satan in the wilderness. These interactions can be compared to the first temptation in the Garden with Adam and Eve (Genesis 3:1-7) and the period of wandering in the wilderness with the nation of Israel. As with Eve, Satan directly approaches an isolated Jesus and challenges what God has said he can and should do. Like Israel's 40 years in the wilderness, Jesus' 40 days include temptation by hunger (Exodus 16:2-8), temptation to test God (Exodus 17:1-4), and temptation of idolatry (Exodus 32). Unlike the temptations with Adam and Eve and the Israelites, Jesus boldly responds with the words of God, quoting Deuteronomy 8:3, 6:16, and 6:13. Unlike Adam and Eve and the Israelites, Jesus doesn't give in to temptation. ▼

Luke's account of the temptations (4:1-13) describes them as a process, a journey by which Satan and Jesus were together. Satan chose three specific times to tempt Jesus, and Jesus responded with truth each time. Satan's power is no match for God's truth.

Share a word or phrase that describes what led up to your shouldn't-have-done-that moment. Why did you do something you knew you weren't supposed to do?

What do these items have to do with sin?

Where in your daily life do you tend to encounter temptation to do something you know you shouldn't do?

GROUNDING

God's Word: Matthew 4:1-11

[1] Then Jesus was led by the Spirit into the wilderness to be tempted by the devil. [2] After fasting forty days and forty nights, he was hungry. [3] The tempter came to him and said, "If you are the Son of God, tell these stones to become bread."

[4] Jesus answered, "It is written: 'Man shall not live on bread alone, but on every word that comes from the mouth of God.'"

[5] Then the devil took him to the holy city and had him stand on the highest point of the temple. [6] "If you are the Son of God," he said, "throw yourself down. For it is written: 'He will command his angels concerning you, and they will lift you up in their hands, so that you will not strike your foot against a stone.'"

[7] Jesus answered him, "It is also written: 'Do not put the Lord your God to the test.'"

[8] Again, the devil took him to a very high mountain and showed him all the kingdoms of the world and their splendor. 9 "All this I will give you," he said, "if you will bow down and worship me."

[10] Jesus said to him, "Away from me, Satan! For it is written: 'Worship the Lord your God, and serve him only.'"

[11] Then the devil left him, and angels came and attended him.

What strikes you about Jesus' encounter with Satan? What questions does it raise for you? Capture those thoughts here.

GRAPPLING

GOING DEEPER

We're all different. Some of us like to speak up, and some of us are more reserved. Some are more familiar with the Bible than others. Some need lots of processing time, and others quickly connect the dots or reach a conclusion. We have different experiences and questions. And…we can learn from one another! Take a deep breath and take it all in. Learn from others, and let others learn from you by asking questions and sharing with respect for others.

Why do you think God allowed Jesus to be tempted by Satan?

Why does Satan think he has any chance to persuade Jesus, the Son of God?

What, if anything, did you discover about resisting temptation from Jesus' responses to temptation?

> ## INTERESTING THOUGHTS SPARKED BY OTHERS IN MY GROUP:

BEHIND THE SCENES

James 1:13 says, "When tempted, no one should say, 'God is tempting me.' For God cannot be tempted by evil, nor does he tempt anyone." So how and why would Jesus be tempted? Remember, words we use slightly differ in meaning depending on the context and the translation. The word translated as "tempted" can also mean "tested." Jesus couldn't and wouldn't sin, and both Satan and the world needed tangible evidence of it. Both had evidence of humans yielding to Satan's temptations before, but Jesus, God in human flesh, succeeded through the testing by knowing, believing, and applying God's Word.

How can Jesus' life leading up to the time of testing, as well as the testing itself, help us when faced with temptations and tests in our own lives?

BEHIND THE SCENES

Jesus uses the words "it is written" three times in Matthew 4:1-11. In fact, Jesus quotes the Old Testament dozens of times in the Gospel of Matthew alone. And Jesus isn't the only one who knows Scripture. Even Satan quotes Psalm 91 in Matthew 4:6. While it's important to know God's Word, it's even more important to live by its guidance.

GROWING

BEHIND THE SCENES

Compare what Satan quotes in Matthew 4:6 with the original words in Psalm 91:11-12.

"If you are the Son of God," he said, "throw yourself down. For it is written: 'He will command his angels concerning you, and they will lift you up in their hands, so that you will not strike your foot against a stone.'" (Matthew 4:6)

"For he will command his angels concerning you to guard you in all your ways; they will lift you up in their hands, so that you will not strike your foot against a stone." (Psalm 91:11-12)

What do you notice about Satan's use of Psalm 91:11-12?

As you cope with temptations in your life, what are ways you can trust God and the truth of God's Word? What might that look like for you?

Write your reflections here.

Throughout this quarter, we'll be exploring the question, Why is Jesus so radical? Based only on what we've discussed today, what's one sentence that might answer that question?

Write your thoughts here.

LESSON 3: WHAT DOES IT REALLY MEAN TO FOLLOW JESUS?

GREETING

BEHIND THE SCENES

When we meet Jesus in Matthew 4:18, he's left Nazareth for Capernaum, and then he continues through Galilee. Verse 23 indicates he taught in synagogues and healed every sickness among the people. His ministry wasn't reserved for those who had the most teaching. It wasn't reserved for Jews. He reached beyond the expectations of others as he connected with the Gentiles. People from many surrounding areas reached out to him, trusting him to teach and heal (verse 25). Jerusalem and Judea were Jewish regions, while Decapolis was primarily Gentiles, and Galilee was a region with a mixture of Jews and Gentiles. Jesus attracted and ministered to them all. He walked among all classes of people. He healed every disease (verse 24). Jesus didn't meet people's expectations. He exceeded them.

How does this challenge the social boundaries of life today?

Extend your arm on a flat surface with your wrist extended just beyond the edge with the index finger and thumb positioned as if they're ready to clamp together and grab something. Your partner will hold the ruler (or other object provided by your leader) vertically above your hand. Make sure the end with zero on it is just above your finger and thumb, but make sure it's not touching. Your partner will drop the ruler, and you should catch it as soon as possible. Write down the centimeter mark from the ruler where your finger and thumb clamp onto the ruler. (If you're using something other than a ruler, just write the approximate length where it was clasped from the end of the object.) Repeat this three times; then switch so that each person gets to test his or her reaction time.

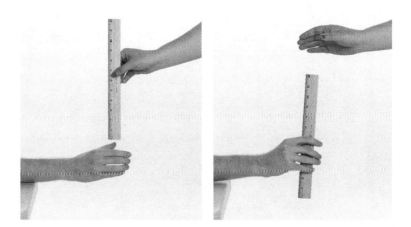

My reaction times:

What surprised—or didn't surprise—you about your reaction time?

When you have the opportunity to lead, what do you expect of those who follow you?

GROUNDING

God's Word: Matthew 4:18-25

[18] As Jesus was walking beside the Sea of Galilee, he saw two brothers, Simon called Peter and his brother Andrew. They were casting a net into the lake, for they were fishermen. [19] "Come, follow me," Jesus said, "and I will send you out to fish for people." [20] At once they left their nets and followed him.

[21] Going on from there, he saw two other brothers, James son of Zebedee and his brother John. They were in a boat with their father Zebedee, preparing their nets. Jesus called them, [22] and immediately they left the boat and their father and followed him.

[23] Jesus went throughout Galilee, teaching in their synagogues, proclaiming the good news of the kingdom, and healing every disease and sickness among the people. [24] News about him spread all over Syria, and people brought to him all who were ill with various diseases, those suffering severe pain, the demon-possessed, those having seizures, and the paralyzed; and he healed them. [25] Large crowds from Galilee, the Decapolis, Jerusalem, Judea and the region across the Jordan followed him.

What are the first questions that come to mind about this passage? What sort of jumps out at you and catches your attention? Capture those thoughts here.

$\checkmark$GRAPPLING

GOING DEEPER

Some questions are left unanswered, and that often makes us uncomfortable. We want to understand. We want the "411." Our desire to understand may cause us to explain something the best we can and call it truth because it's the best we can do. But we're never going to have all the answers. If we did, we'd be equal to God. He wants us to seek him, but let's trust him through the process. God knows what we need to know and when we need to know it.

BEHIND THE SCENES

Matthew 4.18-25 describes Jesus' calling of four men (Simon Peter, Andrew, James, and John) into ministry with him. Jesus didn't wait to see who would come to him. He met them where they were. Jesus didn't go to the Temple and get the experts of the Law to follow him. Jesus knew he needed people who could minister to, relate to, and provide for people in practical ways. He wanted people who could fish, as these men could. He promised them he'd teach them a different kind of fishing, but he would build on what they already knew to develop them into the disciples he knew they could be.

As you read this passage from Matthew, how would you describe the way the disciples followed Jesus?

When Jesus calls followers today, does he expect them to react by dropping everything immediately and following him on the spot? Explain your answer.

INTERESTING THOUGHTS SPARKED
BY OTHERS IN MY GROUP:

BEHIND THE SCENES

This wasn't the first experience Andrew and Simon Peter had with Jesus. Andrew was one of John the Baptist's disciples who encountered Jesus as John identified him as the Lamb of God (John 1:35-40). The first thing Andrew did was tell his brother, Simon Peter, and take him to Jesus, where Simon Peter had his first interaction with Jesus (John 1:41-42).

There are two primary words translated into "know" in our English Bibles. One (*ginōskō*) indicates an insight, awareness, and understanding. It's what God gives us. We might not be aware of every bit of knowledge he's given us, but it's something we don't have to actively learn or experience. He gifts it to us, and it's as if we know it by intuition. The other kind of knowing *(nous)* is what we acquire by learning. We have to experience it somehow—through hearing, reading, doing, and so on—in order to gain the knowledge. Just because we know *about* Jesus doesn't mean we *know* Jesus.

How do you know him?

What does the variety of Jesus' actions and interactions in Matthew 4:18-25 tell you about his ministry—and what it might look like for you to follow Jesus?

GROWING

BEHIND THE SCENES

When Jesus commanded Simon Peter, Andrew, James, and John to follow him, it wasn't a passive invitation. They left what they knew to follow who they wanted to know. Jesus wouldn't just teach them what he knew; he taught them who he was. Following him involved more than accompanying him; it required sacrifice and commitment. It required setting themselves aside and emulating Jesus.

"Then he said to them all: 'Whoever wants to be my disciple must deny themselves and take up their cross daily and follow me. For whoever wants to save their life will lose it, but whoever loses their life for me will save it' "(Luke 9:23-24).

How has your reaction time changed, and why?

Write your observations here.

How would you describe your reaction time to God? What influences how quickly you respond to God?

Write your reflections here.

PARTICIPANT GUIDE

BEHIND THE SCENES

Matthew tells us that the first disciples immediately followed Jesus when he called them. But that immediate response to Jesus' calling didn't mean that they followed him without questions or problems. Far from it. In fact, the Gospels indicate that the disciples wrestled with their commitment, even after Jesus' resurrection from death. Even at the end of Matthew, the 11 remaining disciples went to the mountain where Jesus told them to meet him. When they got there, "they worshipped him; but some doubted" (Matthew 28:17). Nonetheless, Jesus commissioned the disciples to go and make disciples of all nations.

How has a mixture of belief and doubt marked your own discipleship?

As we move through this quarter, we'll continually be wondering on the question, Why is Jesus so radical? Based only on what we've discussed today, what's one sentence that might answer that question?

Write your thoughts here.

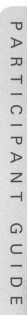

LESSON 4: HOW CAN I TELL IF JESUS CARES ENOUGH TO ACT IN MY SITUATION?

GREETING

Who's a person who has stepped up and met a need of yours? Maybe it was a physical need, an emotional one, or even a financial one. Who was it, and what did that person do for you?

When have you seen a need in someone's life—but decided not to take action because you believed that was actually the better way to help the person?

God's Word: Matthew 9:18-26

[18] While he was saying this, a synagogue leader came and knelt before him and said, "My daughter has just died. But come and put your hand on her, and she will live." [19] Jesus got up and went with him, and so did his disciples.

[20] Just then a woman who had been subject to bleeding for twelve years came up behind him and touched the edge of his cloak. [21] She said to herself, "If I only touch his cloak, I will be healed."

[22] Jesus turned and saw her. "Take heart, daughter," he said, "your faith has healed you." And the woman was healed at that moment.

[23] When Jesus entered the synagogue leader's house and saw the noisy crowd and people playing pipes, [24] he said, "Go away. The girl is not dead but asleep." But they laughed at him. [25] After the crowd had been put outside, he went in and took the girl by the hand, and she got up. [26] News of this spread through all that region.

What are the first questions that come to mind? What jumps out at you and catches your attention? Capture those thoughts here.

$\checkmark$GRAPPLING

GOING DEEPER

Each of us has experienced hurt of some kind. And most of us are compassionate and want to ease other's hurts, which can be a good thing, but we have to know our limits. We can't fix everything. We don't always know the right advice to give someone. Just because we've had a similar experience or we read about a similar experience on Facebook doesn't mean we're experts. Be sensitive when reaching out to others. Focus more on listening than fixing.

BEHIND THE SCENES

Matthew 9:18-26 describes two healings Jesus performs. One is of a woman suffering from a bleeding condition, and the other is the young daughter of a synagogue leader named Jairus. The woman pursues and reaches out to touch Jesus. Jesus goes to the young girl's house and touches her (after the father pursues Jesus). One doesn't have to say a word; the other explains the situation requiring healing. Both the bleeding woman and Jairus display faith that Jesus can heal. Nothing is mentioned about the faith of the young girl herself.

What similarities and what differences do you observe in these healings?

PARTICIPANT GUIDE

What do you discover about Jesus through these two accounts?

INTERESTING THOUGHTS SPARKED
BY OTHERS IN MY GROUP:

BEHIND THE SCENES

A woman who had a bleeding condition would have been considered unclean under Mosaic law, as a woman was considered unclean at any time she was bleeding, including a regular menstrual cycle.

"When a woman has a discharge of blood for many days at a time other than her monthly period or has a discharge that continues beyond her period, she will be unclean as long as she has the discharge, just as in the days of her period. Any bed she lies on while her discharge continues will be unclean, as is her bed during her monthly period, and anything she sits on will be unclean, as during her period. Anyone who touches them will be unclean; they must wash their clothes and bathe with water, and they will be unclean till evening. When she is cleansed from her discharge, she must count off seven days, and after that she will be ceremonially clean" (Leviticus 15:25-28).

An ongoing bleeding condition would have isolated a woman from all regular contact from people, including justifying divorce by her husband. ▶

If someone entered the Temple while unclean, the penalty could range from forty lashes to death by stoning.

Mark's account of this woman adds a detail: "She had suffered a great deal under the care of many doctors and had spent all she had, yet instead of getting better she grew worse" (Mark 5:26). Suffice it to say, she was chronically suffering and desperately wanted healing.

How have you experienced a desperate need for healing—physically, emotionally, relationally, or financially?

How have you experienced faith and doubt side by side?

BEHIND THE SCENES

When Jesus arrives at the synagogue leader Jairus' home, there is a crowd, including people playing pipes, which indicates mourning for the girl is well underway. This isn't a crowd sitting in an intensive care waiting room, fervently praying for a miraculous recovery. This is a funeral home crowd. Jesus' reference to the girl sleeping doesn't indicate a lack of death, as if the mourners don't know the difference between someone who is alive and someone who is dead.

Jesus is referring to a state also referred to in 1 Thessalonians 4:13-14: "Brothers and sisters, we do not want you to be uninformed about those who sleep in death, so that you do not grieve like the rest of mankind, who have no hope. For we believe that Jesus died and rose again, and so we believe that God will bring with Jesus those who have fallen asleep in him."

This type of sleep looks like death to us but is the same state from which believers will be awakened at the time of the final resurrection.

PARTICIPANT GUIDE

GROWING

BEHIND THE SCENES

The story of Jairus and his daughter is also found in the book of Mark, which can give us a little extra insight into the story.

When Jairus first comes to Jesus, his daughter is in the process of dying. Jesus goes with him (Mark 5:22-24). That's when the woman with the bleeding condition, among a large crowd, presses toward him, reaches him, and is healed. Keep in mind that Jairus is still with Jesus. He sees throngs of people slowing Jesus down. He sees Jesus turn around to ask, "Who touched my clothes?" More time passes as Jesus "kept looking around to see who had done it" (Mark 5:32). The woman explains to Jesus that it was her, and they have a conversation. Time continues to pass, and Jairus is still with Jesus when people come to tell him his daughter has died: "'Your daughter is dead,' they said. 'Why bother the teacher anymore?' Overhearing what they said, Jesus told him, 'Don't be afraid; just believe' " (Mark 5:35-36).

Jairus may have thought he'd run out of time, but he hadn't. Still, he had a choice whether or not to continue to believe. Jairus could have gotten angry at the woman who interrupted Jesus' travel to his house. He could have questioned Jesus' intentions for going with him in the first place if Jesus was willing to get delayed by someone else who needed healing. He could have questioned whether or not Jesus cared enough about him to heal his daughter. But Jairus chose to believe instead.

What have I discovered today about knowing if Jesus cares enough to act in my situation? How am I going to respond in fearless faith today?

Write your reflections here.

As we move through this quarter, we'll continually be wondering on the question, Why is Jesus so radical? Based only on what we've discussed today, what's one sentence that might answer that question?

Write your thoughts here.

PARTICIPANT GUIDE

LESSON 4: HOW CAN I TELL IF JESUS CARES 35
ENOUGH TO ACT IN MY SITUATION?

LESSON 5: WHAT DOES IT MEAN IF JESUS REALLY IS GOD'S SON?

GREETING

Even if you don't have what you might consider to be a special talent, what makes you unique?

How would life be different if an important child in your life was a prodigy?

GROUNDING

God's Word: Luke 9:18-36

[18] Once when Jesus was praying in private and his disciples were with him, he asked them, "Who do the crowds say I am?"

[19] They replied, "Some say John the Baptist; others say Elijah; and still others, that one of the prophets of long ago has come back to life."

[20] "But what about you?" he asked. "Who do you say I am?"

Peter answered, "God's Messiah."

[21] Jesus strictly warned them not to tell this to anyone. [22] And he said, "The Son of Man must suffer many things and be rejected by the elders, the chief priests and the teachers of the law, and he must be killed and on the third day be raised to life."

[23] Then he said to them all: "Whoever wants to be my disciple must deny themselves and take up their cross daily and follow me. [24] For whoever wants to save their life will lose it, but whoever loses their life for me will save it. [25] What good is it for someone to gain the whole world, and yet lose or forfeit their very self? [26] Whoever is ashamed of me and my words, the Son of Man will be ashamed of them when he comes in his glory and in the glory of the Father and of the holy angels. ▼

▼

27 "Truly I tell you, some who are standing here will not taste death before they see the kingdom of God."

28 About eight days after Jesus said this, he took Peter, John and James with him and went up onto a mountain to pray. 29 As he was praying, the appearance of his face changed, and his clothes became as bright as a flash of lightning. 30 Two men, Moses and Elijah, appeared in glorious splendor, talking with Jesus. 31 They spoke about his departure, which he was about to bring to fulfillment at Jerusalem. 32 Peter and his companions were very sleepy, but when they became fully awake, they saw his glory and the two men standing with him. 33 As the men were leaving Jesus, Peter said to him, "Master, it is good for us to be here. Let us put up three shelters—one for you, one for Moses and one for Elijah." (He did not know what he was saying.)

34 While he was speaking, a cloud appeared and covered them, and they were afraid as they entered the cloud. 35 A voice came from the cloud, saying, "This is my Son, whom I have chosen; listen to him." 36 When the voice had spoken, they found that Jesus was alone. The disciples kept this to themselves and did not tell anyone at that time what they had seen.

What are the first questions and thoughts that come to mind about this passage? Capture those thoughts here.

✓GRAPPLING

GOING DEEPER

You can help others in your group go deeper by listening with your full attention and by asking questions as others share. Saying "I wonder about what you just said. Tell me more" will help people know you care about what they're saying and want them to open up more. This time is not about "right" and "wrong" answers. It is about questioning, thinking, and exploring the passages.

BEHIND THE SCENES

Luke 9:18-36 represents a major turning point in both Jesus' teaching and people's understanding of who Jesus really is. With Peter's answer to the question, "Who do the crowds say I am?" the question of Jesus' underlying identity is revealed, and Jesus' focus shifts to preparing the disciples for his coming death and their changing responsibilities. In fact, Jesus references his impending suffering six times in Luke (9:22, 44; 12:50; 13:31-33; 17:25; 18:31). Three of the references also have parallels in Mark 8:31-32, 9:30-32, and 10:32-34 (the other three references are unique to Luke's Gospel).

At this point the disciples think this revelation about Jesus and the kingdom of God means there will be an immediate political and military victory on the horizon. Jesus will have to show the disciples that long before there is a final victory, he must face the cross and they will have to adopt lives of sacrificial service. To reiterate this point, the voice from heaven at the place of the Transfiguration tells them to listen to Jesus because he knows the true way to God.

PARTICIPANT GUIDE

If we're honest, we usually think about Jesus as the nice man from the pictures tacked to the wall of our Sunday school rooms. If you were asked the question Jesus asked his followers in Luke 9:20, how would you answer?

What is the significance of Jesus' transfiguration? Why didn't Jesus just come out and tell the disciples who he was from the start?

INTERESTING THOUGHTS SPARKED
BY OTHERS IN MY GROUP:

BEHIND THE SCENES

This was not the only time Jesus shared such a powerful experience with Peter, James, and John. The first time was when he raised Jairus' daughter from the dead (Luke 8:51; Mark 5:37), and the other time was in the Garden of Gethsemane just before his arrest (Mark 14:33). So it was no accident that Jesus selected these particular disciples to ▶

witness his transfiguration. Not only were they three of Jesus' closest friends, but they actually understood more of Jesus' mission and the essence of who he was than anyone else.

BEHIND THE SCENES

It is significant that the Transfiguration took place on a mountain. Many other powerful biblical events took place on mountains. God told Abraham to take his son Isaac to one of the mountains in the region of Moriah and sacrifice him (Genesis 22:2). Moses received the Ten Commandments on Mount Sinai. Elijah the prophet found God's reassuring presence on the same mountain in a "gentle whisper" (1 Kings 19:12). Jesus commissioned the disciples on a mountain. Jesus delivered his most famous sermon on a mountain. In fact, the Gospel of Matthew lists six significant mountain events: Jesus' temptation (4:8); the Sermon on the Mount (5:1); numerous healings (15:29-30); the Transfiguration (17:1); Jesus' foretelling of the destruction of the Temple and the signs of the end times (24:1); and the commissioning of the disciples (28:16).

GROWING

BEHIND THE SCENES

Jesus' refusal of Peter's desire to build a tabernacle is more than just a reaction to the disciple's exuberance. It is a tangible reminder that revelation and inspiration have a purpose. They are to be expressed in both inward reflection and outward acts of ministry and service.

When have you had a "mountain-top experience" where you felt God in a powerful way? How did you react?

Write your reflections here.

BEHIND THE SCENES

The Transfiguration is a moment full of mystery and supernatural phenomena, with the voice speaking from the cloud (a biblical symbol for God). That's interesting because of its imagery. After the exodus from Egypt, a cloud led the Israelites on their journey to the Promised Land. And in Acts when Jesus ascended to heaven, he did so through a cloud.

If Jesus is the Messiah, God's Son, what does that mean for my life?

Write your thoughts here.

This quarter we're grappling with the question, Why is Jesus so radical? Based only on what we've discussed today, what's one sentence that might answer that question?

Record your reflections here.

LESSON 6: WHY DID JESUS TELL SUCH CONFUSING STORIES?

GREETING

Why are stories—about our lives or anything else—important?

GROUNDING

God's Word: Matthew 13:24-45

24 Jesus told them another parable: "The kingdom of heaven is like a man who sowed good seed in his field. 25 But while everyone was sleeping, his enemy came and sowed weeds among the wheat, and went away. 26 When the wheat sprouted and formed heads, then the weeds also appeared.

27 "The owner's servants came to him and said, 'Sir, didn't you sow good seed in your field? Where then did the weeds come from?' ▼

▼

28 "'An enemy did this,' he replied.

"The servants asked him, 'Do you want us to go and pull them up?'

29 "'No,' he answered, 'because while you are pulling the weeds, you may uproot the wheat with them. 30 Let both grow together until the harvest. At that time I will tell the harvesters: First collect the weeds and tie them in bundles to be burned; then gather the wheat and bring it into my barn.'"

31 He told them another parable: "The kingdom of heaven is like a mustard seed, which a man took and planted in his field. 32 Though it is the smallest of all seeds, yet when it grows, it is the largest of garden plants and becomes a tree, so that the birds come and perch in its branches."

33 He told them still another parable: "The kingdom of heaven is like yeast that a woman took and mixed into about sixty pounds of flour until it worked all through the dough."

34 Jesus spoke all these things to the crowd in parables; he did not say anything to them without using a parable. 35 So was fulfilled what was spoken through the prophet:

"I will open my mouth in parables,

I will utter things hidden since the creation of the world."

36 Then he left the crowd and went into the house. His disciples came to him and said, "Explain to us the parable of the weeds in the field."

37 He answered, "The one who sowed the good seed is the Son of Man. 38 The field is the world, and the good seed stands for the people of the kingdom. The weeds are the people of the evil one, 39 and the enemy who sows them is the devil. The harvest is the end of the age, and the harvesters are angels.

40 "As the weeds are pulled up and burned in the fire, so it will be at the end of the age. 41 The Son of Man will send out his angels, and they will weed out of his kingdom everything that causes sin and all who do evil. 42 They will throw them into the blazing furnace, where there will be weeping and gnashing of teeth. 43 Then the righteous will shine like the sun in the kingdom of their Father. Whoever has ears, let them hear." ▶

[44] "The kingdom of heaven is like treasure hidden in a field. When a man found it, he hid it again, and then in his joy went and sold all he had and bought that field. [45] "Again, the kingdom of heaven is like a merchant looking for fine pearls."

Does anything strike you as unusual or interesting about these parables? Would they hold the attention of a modern audience (why or why not)? Capture your thoughts here.

GRAPPLING

GOING DEEPER

We live in a sound-bite world. Our attention is captured by quick videos, brief emails, and a quick text or two. We look and then we move on, often comprehending on a surface level at best. So let's make this time and place together different. Let's make an effort to be engaged with each other, saying things like "What a wonderful insight. Keep going!" Let's share our stories and the truths behind our stories.

BEHIND THE SCENES

The parables (and corresponding concepts) in Matthew 13:24-45 were a departure from the norm for the people of Jesus' day. He was using a new form of communication to deliver a new kind of message; something very different from what they were accustomed to hearing. ▼

These were stories that engaged the people listening in every aspect of their lives. And they were *secular* stories. Stories about land, livestock, treasures, money, food, occupations. Things the people understood. But the amazing thing is that these stories were designed to move the listener from a world they were familiar with to a world filled with hope and promise. A world where peace and justice were the standard.

For example, in the parable of the weeds, Jesus talked about a world they were familiar with: The world of agriculture. But in talking about a sower who scattered his seeds in a field (just as many of them had done themselves), the emphasis moves subtly from the day-to-day trials of a farmer to the reality of two kingdoms set squarely against one another. And it leaves the hearer with a question: *What kind of seed am I?*

Parables were a stark reminder that the things the people had grown comfortable with were not necessarily trustworthy and sometimes our efforts to right a wrong simply make things worse (pulling the wheat with the weeds). And by following God's direction we see that evil is temporary and good ultimately endures.

Though Jesus was talking directly to the people with him, he's also talking to us through these parables. What message do you find in the parables we've read?

BEHIND THE SCENES

In this passage, Jesus describes a kingdom that is in the present and in the future. The Kingdom is here, but it is not entirely here yet. We are confronted by the reality of the Kingdom in the present. But we will only experience God's kingdom fully when it comes in the future. Notice that Jesus says, "The kingdom is at hand."

The parables were designed to show this present/future connection. Each parable is a multi-layered story. In the parable of the weeds, the weeds are a problem now but the ultimate solution can only come about through future actions.

This section also shows us something about Jesus himself and the importance of his message. Even though Jesus knew that many people would not receive him and many would reject him, he shared his message and his life with them and continued to minister to them with compassion.

INTERESTING THOUGHTS SPARKED BY OTHERS IN MY GROUP:

BEHIND THE SCENES

In the parable of the mustard seed, Jesus used one of the smallest seeds known to his audience to illustrate a very big point. The plant that grows from the tiny mustard seed can grow to be between 8 to 10 feet tall around the Lake of Galilee. This fact vividly illustrated Jesus' point that the small can become mighty.

Jesus used illustrations from everyday life to make his point. In what other ways were the parables meant to be effective.

Based on these parables, what do you think the kingdom of heaven is like?

Can someone who does not believe that Jesus is God's Son still understand the message of the Bible?

PARTICIPANT GUIDE

GROWING

BEHIND THE SCENES

While the parables were meant to reveal hidden principles and truths, there was also hidden truth in the actions of Christ himself. Matthew's Gospel depicts Jesus as the Messiah, and the scenes Matthew favors are those that symbolically portray Jesus as a king interacting with his subjects. Not an aloof, power-wielding king showing off for the people, but a benevolent ruler making himself known and forming relationships with the ones he came to bring the kingdom of heaven to.

How were the people of Galilee who heard these parables like or unlike us today? More specifically, how do you see yourself in them?

Write your reflections here.

As we move through this quarter, we'll continually be exploring the question, Why is Jesus so radical? Based only on what we've discussed today, what's one sentence that might answer that question?

Write your thoughts here.

LESSON 7: WAS JESUS RACIST, OR SEXIST—OR BOTH?

GREETING

When it comes to the person I am closest to, I have faith that...

When it comes to God, I have faith that...

Why do you think faith is important in a relationship—whether with God or with a person?

GROUNDING

God's Word: Matthew 15:21-28

[21] Leaving that place, Jesus withdrew to the region of Tyre and Sidon. [22] A Canaanite woman from that vicinity came to him, crying out, "Lord, Son of David, have mercy on me! My daughter is demon-possessed and suffering terribly."

[23] Jesus did not answer a word. So his disciples came to him and urged him, "Send her away, for she keeps crying out after us."

[24] He answered, "I was sent only to the lost sheep of Israel."

[25] The woman came and knelt before him. "Lord, help me!" she said.

[26] He replied, "It is not right to take the children's bread and toss it to the dogs."

[27] "Yes it is, Lord," she said. "Even the dogs eat the crumbs that fall from their master's table."

[28] Then Jesus said to her, "Woman, you have great faith! Your request is granted." And her daughter was healed at that moment.

What jumps out at you and catches your attention in this passage? What questions do you have? Capture those thoughts here.

GRAPPLING

GOING DEEPER

Remember that just as you are responsible for your own learning, you can also play an important role in the faith journey of others. You can help others in your group go deeper by listening with your full attention and by asking questions as others share. Make this an interactive time together. Encouraging others will help people know you care about what they're saying and may help them to open up more.

BEHIND THE SCENES

Matthew 15:21-28 can be a little hard to hear if we take it at face value. On the surface, a woman approaches Jesus and he makes her all but beg for her daughter's healing. But on closer inspection we see this as another turning point in Jesus' ministry. In verse 24 he says, "I was sent only to the lost sheep of Israel." And in this instance he was talking about Israel in general. As it says in Isaiah 53:6, "We all, like sheep, have gone astray, each of us has turned to our own way; and the Lord has laid on him the iniquity of us all." Jesus' mission was originally to reveal himself as the Messiah they were expecting.

But there was something in the persistent faith of the Canaanite woman that touched Jesus. She humbles herself to the point of saying even the dogs get scraps from their masters' tables, and Jesus cannot refuse her. She has recognized him as the Messiah and approaches him with faith and reverence.

What's your response to the Jesus we meet in this passage, and why?

Why would Jesus need to test anyone's faith? And in what ways do you think Jesus tests our faith today, if ever?

INTERESTING THOUGHTS SPARKED
BY OTHERS IN MY GROUP:

BEHIND THE SCENES

Was Jesus racist? As we come into the scene, Jesus has taken some time to rest. But the place he has stopped to recharge is in the land of the Canaanites. They were in many ways the biblical enemies of Israel because their paganism had often led Israel into idolatry. If Jesus was a racist, it seems unlikely that he would choose to stop and relax in a place where there was animosity.

It's possible that he went to the region of Tyre and Sidon because that is the last place people would expect a Jew to go. Or what other reasons might Jesus have had for choosing this location as a rest stop?

GROWING

Tell about a time you persevered in your faith, or perhaps you are in a situation like this right now that you're willing to share about.

Pray with your small group, thanking God for helping us to persevere in difficult times. If there is anyone in your group who is going through a time of persevering right now, be sure to pray specifically for that person.

BEHIND THE SCENES

Was Jesus sexist? Let's face it; he called the woman a dog. Or did he?

In this instance Jesus is referring to Jews as children and to Gentiles as dogs. Not the wild, feral dogs that roamed the land, but the mild-mannered house dogs. Jesus used this comparison to allude to his mission and to show the Jews he was the Messiah. Jesus makes a similar reference in Mark 7:27, " 'First let the children eat all they want,' he told her, 'for it is not right to take the children's bread and toss it to the dogs.' " And the Canaanite woman, who called Jesus "Lord" through the whole exchange, was not offended by the reference because she understood who Jesus was. And she also understood that he was her daughter's only hope.

The faith he was hoping to instill in the Jews was vital and alive in this Gentile woman. And because of her faith, his mission enlarged to include the Gentiles. In other words, she was the mom who changed the world.

PARTICIPANT GUIDE

Just as Jesus ultimately extended grace, mercy, and healing to the woman and her daughter, God also extends those to you. Where do you need to experience grace, mercy, or healing?

Write your reflections as a prayer to God.

As we move through this quarter, we'll continually be wondering on the question, Why is Jesus so radical? Based only on what we've discussed today, what's one sentence that might answer that question?

Write your thoughts here.

LESSON 8: WHAT'S JESUS GOT AGAINST GROWN-UPS?

GREETING

Are you usually happy to babysit, or does it feel like an imposition? Share why you answer as you do.

If all you had to judge society's attitude toward children was a copy of the TV Guide, what conclusions might you come up with?

If you visited a nice restaurant and had to make conclusions about the role of children in society based on what you saw, what opinions might you form?

If a stranger visited our church and walked around, what would he or she say about how we valued children?

BEHIND THE SCENES

Jesus was a master at radically turning over "sacred conventions" and assumptions, offering a new way to relate to God and others. Children in the Old Testament were valued and a sign of blessing for their parents, who gained honor and prestige as their family grew. There was nothing wrong with that, but Jesus "flipped" that idea by saying that the honor of children is not in what they provide for parents, but how they approach God in total humility. In a similar way, Jesus "flips" the idea of patriarchal honor and privilege in the parable of the prodigal son (Luke 15:11-32). One scholar says the title should be the "Parable of the Crazy Father," since the father does everything "wrong" according to long-held customs in regard to both his sons. Yet Jesus clearly indicates that God is like the crazy father in the parable.

What other things did Jesus "flip" in his ministry?

GROUNDING

God's Word: Luke 18:15-17

[15] People were also bringing babies to Jesus for him to place his hands on them. When the disciples saw this, they rebuked them. [16] But Jesus called the children to him and said, "Let the little children come to me, and do not hinder them, for the kingdom of God belongs to such as these. [17] Truly I tell you, anyone who will not receive the kingdom of God like a little child will never enter it."

When you read this passage, what jumps out at you and grabs your attention? Write down your thoughts here.

BEHIND THE SCENES

The image of becoming a child seemed to be Jesus' metaphor of choice when attempting to convince those in the religious establishment that their system of good works and adherence to their strict interpretation of the law of Moses did nothing to make them worthy of being citizens of God's kingdom. In John 3, Nicodemus, a Pharisee, makes a midnight visit to Jesus to secretly inquire how to become right with God. Nicodemus wasn't an average Pharisee. John describes him as "Israel's teacher." He knew the Mosaic law inside and out and had the reputation of being a prominent authority on the topic. Jesus responded to him by telling him he needed to be reborn from above. Nicodemus was perfectly powerless, despite his impressive religious pedigree. ▼

Many theologians believe Nicodemus placed his faith in God, although in secret due to his position, since he reappears at the end of John's Gospel to assist with Jesus' burial.

GRAPPLING

BEHIND THE SCENES

This week's account is short—only three verses long—but it's enough to reveal Jesus' inclusiveness when it comes to who can participate in his kingdom. Some scholars believe the concept of childhood wasn't as fully formed in Bible times as it is today. Children were marginalized until they were old enough to contribute to the greater good. The text in the original language reveals that the parents were bringing infants and toddlers to Jesus, so these were the least valuable of people, according to the culture at the time. Mothers didn't bond with their children as strongly as mothers and children bond today due to the high infant and child mortality rates. The Romans—Israel's oppressors—routinely exposed unwanted children to the elements. This practice was prohibited, but it's clear from this passage that children didn't enjoy the same social status as adults. An onlooker could have seen Jesus' behavior and decided that if he had time for children, then he had time for anyone.

But Jesus goes a step further and lifts children up as an example of what someone needs to be like in order to enter God's kingdom. He doesn't specify how we need to be like children, but instead leaves it for his disciples to struggle with.

Why do you think the disciples scolded the parents of the children? What could be their reasoning for this?

Why do you think Jesus held up children as a positive role model for what it means to be able to receive the kingdom of heaven?

GOING DEEPER

Remember, the measure of a fearless conversation isn't whether or not you convince others of your opinions concerning the Bible. A fearless conversation is successful when the group collectively grows closer to God and each other.

INTERESTING THOUGHTS SPARKED
BY OTHERS IN MY GROUP:

PARTICIPANT GUIDE

BEHIND THE SCENES

Sandwich-ing: Sometimes Luke intentionally puts one passage in the middle of two others to make a point. Our account is "sandwiched" between a parable and the account of a rich ruler who wanted to know how to enter the kingdom of heaven. This sandwiching of accounts lets us see three different responses to Jesus and consider which response Jesus honors most. If you want greater context for today's reading, dig into this entire chapter in Luke for more!

GROWING

How do you view your relationship with Jesus? In what ways do you approach Jesus as a trusting child, and in what ways do you remind yourself of the scolding disciples?

Write your thoughts here.

What is one step (even a "baby" step) you could take to relate more deeply as a child of God?

Record your thoughts here.

This quarter we're grappling with the question, Why is Jesus so radical? Based only on what we've discussed today, what's one sentence that might answer that question?

Write your reflections here.

LESSON 9: WHAT WAS REALLY GOING ON AT JESUS' "TRIUMPHAL ENTRY" INTO JERUSALEM?

GREETING

The most polarizing people we can think of:

Strongly Dislike   Strongly Like

GOING DEEPER

Don't allow yourself to get baited into a debate over the merit of a particular celebrity or politician. It's enough to agree that people have sharp opposing opinions about that person.

What would it be like to be that polarizing person? How would you deal with the pressure of being under so much scrutiny?

On a scale of 1 to 10, how polarizing is Jesus in our culture? Why?

BEHIND THE SCENES

In Luke, Jesus resisted allowing others to publically identify himself up to this point. After healing someone, he would often send that person off with strict instructions to tell no one. Jesus possessed a keen awareness that "his time had not yet come." But now, he chooses to enter Jerusalem in a choreographed manner that seems to encourage a response from the crowds. Now he allows the crowds to publically adore him as the Christ. He is forcing everyone to have an opinion about him. He chose to enter Jerusalem when it was teaming with Jewish pilgrims, who were returning from all over the known world to celebrate the Passover. Historians note that Jerusalem's streets were barely passable. This was the moment for his grand entrance.

The Old Testament prophet Zechariah predicted that Israel's Messiah and rightful King would enter the Holy City with gentleness and humility, riding on a donkey (Zechariah 9:9). This modest entrance would stand out, as it was customary for conquering rulers of the day to enter a ▼

newly defeated city on a proud war horse. Jesus carefully fulfilled the prophecy in a way that both symbolically fulfilled the prophecy and signaled the nature of his kingship.

Although this passage is commonly referred to as "The Triumphal Entry," Luke doesn't continue the narrative long enough for Jesus to enter the city. He was on the move, riding and forcing everyone around him to make a choice about who he is.

The crowds who had followed his teaching and healing ministry turned out to greet Jesus on the way and publically adore him as their King. The crowds openly received Jesus as their rightful ruler. They were so convinced Jesus was the Chosen One, who would use military force to drive out their oppressors, they were unbothered by the fact that armed Roman soldiers were stationed inside Jerusalem's walls.

The Pharisees, however, were quite bothered by the public demonstration. They approached Jesus and demanded he silence his followers, presumably to keep them from calling down the wrath of their Roman oppressors. But Jesus is very clear: The time had arrived for Jerusalem to recognize their rightful King. Stones would declare the truth if necessary.

GROUNDING

God's Word: Luke 19:28-40

[28] After telling this story, Jesus went on toward Jerusalem, walking ahead of his disciples. [29] As he came to the towns of Bethphage and Bethany on the Mount of Olives, he sent two disciples ahead. [30] "Go into that village over there," he told them. "As you enter it, you will see a young donkey tied there that no one has ever ridden. Untie it and bring it here. [31] If anyone asks, 'Why are you untying that colt?' just say, 'The Lord needs it.'"

[32] So they went and found the colt, just as Jesus had said. [33] And sure enough, as they were untying it, the owners asked them, "Why are you untying that colt?"

[34] And the disciples simply replied, "The Lord needs it." [35] So they brought the colt to Jesus and threw their garments over it for him to ride on.

[36] As he rode along, the crowds spread out their garments on the road ahead of him. [37] When he reached the place where the road started down the Mount of Olives, all of his followers began to shout and sing as they walked along, praising God for all the wonderful miracles they had seen.

[38] "Blessings on the King who comes in the name of the Lord! Peace in heaven, and glory in highest heaven!"

[39] But some of the Pharisees among the crowd said, "Teacher, rebuke your followers for saying things like that!"

[40] He replied, "If they kept quiet, the stones along the road would burst into cheers!"

PARTICIPANT GUIDE

What questions immediately come to mind? What gets your attention? Capture those thoughts here.

GRAPPLING

GOING DEEPER

You can help your group go deeper by how you handle disagreements. If you have a difference of opinion with someone, saying, "I'm not sure I agree. Can you help me understand?" goes a long way to show you respect their opinion, even if you don't share it.

What risks were the crowds taking by singing that Jesus was the king who came in God's name? What do you think emboldened them to take this risk?

What do you think was behind Jesus' comment that in this moment he would be declared King, even if the rocks needed to do the work?

BEHIND THE SCENES

From our present-day vantage point and the benefit of hindsight, it's very easy for us to look at the Pharisees as the villains of the story. However, the Pharisees were viewed much more positively in Jesus' day. The Jews were living in the aftermath of Roman occupation as judgment for their disobedience of their covenant with God. The Pharisees, with their emphasis on rule keeping, were seen as the protectors of Israel's moral standing before God. In a sense, they were actively securing their country's national security. By strictly following God's rules, they hoped God would in turn renew the covenant and then intervene to remove Roman oppression.

Is it possible for people have a "neutral" opinion about Jesus today? Why or why not?

INTERESTING THOUGHTS SPARKED
BY OTHERS IN MY GROUP:

GROWING

So where are you at? Are you like the crowds, who like the promise of Jesus so much that you are trying to enroll him in your cause? Are you like the Pharisees in that you aren't convinced Jesus is who he says he is? Or are you like the Romans who perceive Jesus as a threat to the way you like to rule your own life?

Or perhaps you are like Jesus' disciples—you've committed to follow him, and you know you have more to learn about what he is truly like.

Reflect on these options and write your thoughts about where you are right now.

We're answering the question "Why is Jesus so radical?" this quarter. Based only on what we've discussed today, what's one sentence that might answer that question?

Write your reflections here.

EARLESS
ONVERSATION™

WHY IS
JESUS SO
RADICAL?

PARTICIPANT GUIDE

LESSON 10: WHAT IF GOD WANTS MORE THAN I WANT TO GIVE?

GREETING

What house rules were the hardest for you to obey when you were growing up? Why?

GOING DEEPER

Look around to see if there's anyone new in class. If so, be sure to offer that person a warm welcome and help them feel at home.

BEHIND THE SCENES

Today's passage is a study in contrasts between Jesus and his disciples and how well they obeyed. God wanted more from them than they wanted to give. Jesus was aware he was about to be betrayed at the hand of Judas, an event that would ultimately lead to his death on the cross and his experiencing separation from his Heavenly Father. The latter consequence was infinitely more severe than the first. From eternity, Jesus was a member of the Trinity and experienced a perfect and intimate relationship with the Father and the Holy Spirit. This closeness would be broken when Jesus bore the sins of the world. When Jesus hung on the cross, he responded to this alienation by asking why God had forsaken him.

Before then, in the Garden of Gethsemane, Jesus bore the anxiety that came with anticipating his fate. He asked Peter, James, and John to join him in prayer as he asked God for the strength to obey. In this time of prayer, Jesus wasn't shrinking from his impending death. Instead, he suffered knowing that he alone would bear God's anger that the world earned due to its sinfulness. Jesus asked God to take this burden from him, but he qualified his request by adding he would surrender to God's will instead of his own.

GROUNDING

God's Word: Matthew 26:36-55

[36] Then Jesus went with them to the olive grove called Gethsemane, and he said, "Sit here while I go over there to pray." [37] He took Peter and Zebedee's two sons, James and John, and he became anguished and distressed. [38] He told them, "My soul is crushed with grief to the point of death. Stay here and keep watch with me."

[39] He went on a little farther and bowed with his face to the ground, praying, "My Father! If it is possible, let this cup of suffering be taken away from me. Yet I want your will to be done, not mine."

[40] Then he returned to the disciples and found them asleep. He said to Peter, "Couldn't you watch with me even one hour? [41] Keep watch ▶

and pray, so that you will not give in to temptation. For the spirit is willing, but the body is weak!"

[42] Then Jesus left them a second time and prayed, "My Father! If this cup cannot be taken away unless I drink it, your will be done." [43] When he returned to them again, he found them sleeping, for they couldn't keep their eyes open.

[44] So he went to pray a third time, saying the same things again. [45] Then he came to the disciples and said, "Go ahead and sleep. Have your rest. But look—the time has come. The Son of Man is betrayed into the hands of sinners. [46] Up, let's be going. Look, my betrayer is here!"

[47] While he was still speaking, Judas, one of the Twelve, arrived. With him was a large crowd armed with swords and clubs, sent from the chief priests and the elders of the people. [48] Now the betrayer had arranged a signal with them: "The one I kiss is the man; arrest him." [49] Going at once to Jesus, Judas said, "Greetings, Rabbi!" and kissed him.

[50] Jesus replied, "Do what you came for, friend."

Then the men stepped forward, seized Jesus and arrested him. [51] With that, one of Jesus' companions reached for his sword, drew it out and struck the servant of the high priest, cutting off his ear.

[52] "Put your sword back in its place," Jesus said to him, "for all who draw the sword will die by the sword. [53] Do you think I cannot call on my Father, and he will at once put at my disposal more than twelve legions of angels? [54] But how then would the Scriptures be fulfilled that say it must happen in this way?"

[55] In that hour Jesus said to the crowd, "Am I leading a rebellion, that you have come out with swords and clubs to capture me? Every day I sat in the temple courts teaching, and you did not arrest me.

What questions come to mind and what catches your attention in this passage? Capture those thoughts here.

$\check{G}$RAPPLING

Jesus was fully God yet still struggled to want to obey his Father. In what ways does that remind you of yourself?

GOING DEEPER

If you notice someone in your group taking up all the discussion time, consider asking one of your other group members what they think. (You don't have to be the leader to ask someone what he or she thinks.) Always be looking for ways to include everyone in the conversation.

BEHIND THE SCENES

Throughout the Bible, the number "three" signifies completeness. Jesus wrestled with God in prayer three times and completely surrendered to God. The disciples surrendered to sleep three times and were completely unprepared to resist the temptation to resist arrest through violence.

What difference does it make whether the disciples were asleep or not, given the certainty of Jesus' arrest and crucifixion?

GROWING

Jesus trusted his Father enough to tell him that he didn't want to obey, even while affirming that he would. He had confidence in his Father and trusted him with this honesty.

What might I take from Jesus' example that can help me be obedient to God even when I feel like God is asking too much from me?

Write your reflections here.

Write out a prayer to God about an area in your life where you find it difficult to obey him.

This quarter we're considering the question, Why is Jesus so radical? Based only on what we've discussed today, what's one sentence that might answer that question?

Write your reflections here.

LESSON 11:
DID GOD REALLY DISOWN JESUS ON THE CROSS?

GREETING

What group did you most associate with in high school, and why?

Was being labeled as a part of this group positive, or did you feel like an outcast in this group? Explain your answer.

God's Word: Matthew 27:32-55

[32] As they were going out, they met a man from Cyrene, named Simon, and they forced him to carry the cross. [33] They came to a place called Golgotha (which means "the place of the skull"). [34] There they offered Jesus wine to drink, mixed with gall; but after tasting it, he refused to drink it. [35] When they had crucified him, they divided up his clothes by casting lots. [36] And sitting down, they kept watch over him there. [37] Above his head they placed the written charge against him: THIS IS JESUS, THE KING OF THE JEWS.

[38] Two rebels were crucified with him, one on his right and one on his left. [39] Those who passed by hurled insults at him, shaking their heads [40] and saying, "You who are going to destroy the temple and build it in three days, save yourself! Come down from the cross, if you are the Son of God!" [41] In the same way the chief priests, the teachers of the law and the elders mocked him. [42] "He saved others," they said, "but he can't save himself! He's the king of Israel! Let him come down now from the cross, and we will believe in him. [43] He trusts in God. Let God rescue him now if he wants him, for he said, 'I am the Son of God.'" [44] In the same way the rebels who were crucified with him also heaped insults on him.

[45] From noon until three in the afternoon darkness came over all the land. [46] About three in the afternoon Jesus cried out in a loud voice, *"Eli, Eli, lema sabachthani?"* (which means "My God, my God, why have you forsaken me?")

[47] When some of those standing there heard this, they said, "He's calling Elijah."

[48] Immediately one of them ran and got a sponge. He filled it with wine vinegar, put it on a staff, and offered it to Jesus to drink. [49] The rest said, "Now leave him alone. Let's see if Elijah comes to save him."

[50] And when Jesus had cried out again in a loud voice, he gave up his spirit.

[51] At that moment the curtain of the temple was torn in two from top to bottom. The earth shook, the rocks split [52] and the tombs broke open. The bodies of many holy people who had died were raised to life. [53] They came out of the tombs after Jesus' resurrection and went into the holy city and appeared to many people.

[54] When the centurion and those with him who were guarding Jesus saw the earthquake and all that had happened, they were terrified, and exclaimed, "Surely he was the Son of God!"

[55] Many women were there, watching from a distance. They had followed Jesus from Galilee to care for his needs.

When you read this passage, what jumps out at you and grabs your attention? Write down your thoughts here.

BEHIND THE SCENES

The word *excruciating* comes from the same root word for crucifixion— and for good reason. This finely-tuned method of torture and execution had been perfected by the Romans to maximize the mental, emotional, and physical agony of the condemned person. It was not uncommon for the Romans to crucify more than one person at a time. In fact, the roads leading up to Jerusalem had hundreds of crosses along them, set apart like telephone poles, with those being crucified at various stages of death—the process of which would sometimes last for days.

The public display of a crucified man was meant to maximize the humiliation of this person, who had been stripped then roped and nailed to a wooden beam, which had already been stained with the blood and bodily fluids of previous victims. There is simply no more agonizing picture of the total rejection of a human being than to crucify that individual during this time in history. The ultimate cruelty of crucifixion was the creation of a state of complete hopelessness in the victim.

PARTICIPANT GUIDE

GRAPPLING

What kind of gut reaction do you have when you read the account of Jesus' crucifixion?

GOING DEEPER

As people in your groups share stories about difficult personal experiences, do your best to empathize with what they're saying, either by sharing a similar story of your own or validating how they must have felt. Of course, be careful not to minimize the impact of their challenging event by saying something along the lines of "Oh you think that's bad...I can top that!"

How do you think the crowd's reaction to Jesus' crucifixion would have added to his sense of humiliation and rejection?

INTERESTING THOUGHTS SPARKED
BY OTHERS IN MY GROUP:

BEHIND THE SCENES

Matthew's account of the Crucifixion gives us clues about what happened to Jesus without explicitly saying so. Jesus needed help carrying the cross, probably because his whipping had been so severe his shredded muscles simply couldn't bear the weight of the beam. Jesus refused the gall-infused wine because it was used as a painkiller for the crucified, one of the few merciful options offered to those who were about to die in this hideous manner. Jesus refused the sedative, however, because he needed to bear the full brunt of the sacrifice he made willingly. The fact that the soldiers were divvying up his clothes tells us that Jesus was probably stripped down to his loin cloth or was even naked, again to increase the humiliation of the experience.

What do you think was the significance of all the miraculous events that occurred in the moments surrounding Christ's death?

BEHIND THE SCENES

Matthew calls attention to the detail that the curtain in the Temple, which protected the Holy of Holies, was torn from top to bottom—and not the reverse. From this the reader can conclude that it was God doing the tearing (not two people at the bottom pulling the two sides apart). With the curtain torn in two, people now had full access to the Holy of Holies, which represented God's presence.

What do you think is the connection between God tearing this curtain in two and Jesus' atoning work on the cross?

GROWING

PARTICIPANT GUIDE

What does it mean to me personally to know that Jesus is the Son of God? What does this mean in my own life?

Write your thoughts here.

As we've moved through this quarter, we've been working through the question, Why is Jesus so radical? Based only on what we've discussed today, what's one sentence that might answer that question?

Write your thoughts here.

LESSON 12:
RESURRECTION SEEMS SO IMPOSSIBLE... HOW CAN I BELIEVE IN A LITERAL "EASTER" STORY?

GREETING

What do you think you're good at recognizing as a fake? Money? Artwork? Watches? Designer clothing? How do you know something is fake?

PARTICIPANT GUIDE

LESSON 12: RESURRECTION SEEMS SO IMPOSSIBLE... HOW CAN I BELIEVE IN A LITERAL "EASTER" STORY?

81

Tell about a time you heard a rumor and, for at least a while, you believed it was true. What made the rumor so believable at the time?

GROUNDING

God's Word: Matthew 27:62–28:15

[62] The next day, the one after Preparation Day, the chief priests and the Pharisees went to Pilate. [63] "Sir," they said, "we remember that while he was still alive that deceiver said, 'After three days I will rise again.' [64] So give the order for the tomb to be made secure until the third day. Otherwise, his disciples may come and steal the body and tell the people that he has been raised from the dead. This last deception will be worse than the first."

[65] "Take a guard," Pilate answered. "Go, make the tomb as secure as you know how." [66] So they went and made the tomb secure by putting a seal on the stone and posting the guard.

28 After the Sabbath, at dawn on the first day of the week, Mary Magdalene and the other Mary went to look at the tomb.

[2] There was a violent earthquake, for an angel of the Lord came down from heaven and, going to the tomb, rolled back the stone and sat on it. [3] His appearance was like lightning, and his clothes were white as snow. [4] The guards were so afraid of him that they shook and became like dead men.

[5] The angel said to the women, "Do not be afraid, for I know that you are looking for Jesus, who was crucified. [6] He is not here; he has ▶

risen, just as he said. Come and see the place where he lay. [7] Then go quickly and tell his disciples: 'He has risen from the dead and is going ahead of you into Galilee. There you will see him.' Now I have told you."

[8] So the women hurried away from the tomb, afraid yet filled with joy, and ran to tell his disciples. [9] Suddenly Jesus met them. "Greetings," he said. They came to him, clasped his feet and worshiped him. [10] Then Jesus said to them, "Do not be afraid. Go and tell my brothers to go to Galilee; there they will see me."

[11] While the women were on their way, some of the guards went into the city and reported to the chief priests everything that had happened. [12] When the chief priests had met with the elders and devised a plan, they gave the soldiers a large sum of money, [13] telling them, "You are to say, 'His disciples came during the night and stole him away while we were asleep.' [14] If this report gets to the governor, we will satisfy him and keep you out of trouble." [15] So the soldiers took the money and did as they were instructed. And this story has been widely circulated among the Jews to this very day."

What questions come to mind? What catches your attention? Capture those thoughts here.

BEHIND THE SCENES

Even the enemies of Jesus remembered his prediction that after three days he would rise from the dead. So the religious leaders and the Romans took every precaution possible to be certain that the disciples (who were hiding in fear for their own lives) wouldn't sneak in and steal the body. Pilate gave instructions to make the tomb as secure as possible. This meant a seal and a guard. If anyone attempted to break a Roman seal without authorization, that person would be crucified immediately. The guards themselves would be crucified if they allowed anyone to do it without a fight to the death. In fact, tradition tells us that the soldiers guarding the tomb were crucified themselves for failing to keep Jesus' body in the tomb.

As Jesus reminded Pilate, the governor would have no authority unless it had been given to him by God. So God had no problem superseding the authority of the Roman seal and telling his angelic messengers to simply go break it so that the Risen Christ could walk out of the tomb unhindered. After the Resurrection, Jesus simply appeared and disappeared, so he probably didn't need the stone rolled away.

But those who would be the first witnesses of the Resurrection certainly did.

GRAPPLING

What problems did the religious leaders who pushed for Jesus' crucifixion believe his death would solve? What problems did they discover still remained?

What do you think is the importance of establishing more than one eyewitness here?

GOING DEEPER

When the women heard the news that Jesus had risen from the dead, they were filled with mixed emotions (the text says they were "afraid yet filled with joy"). The people in your group may get emotional during your discussion. Sometimes spiritual growth is messy. As long as they stay respectful of you and others, allow the people in your group whatever room they need to express how they really feel.

INTERESTING THOUGHTS SPARKED BY OTHERS IN MY GROUP:

BEHIND THE SCENES

More than likely, the two Marys followed the angel's instructions, stepping over the heavily armed unconscious guards and looking into the tomb to find it empty. If the women had arrived any earlier, they would have probably been cut down immediately by the guards whose own lives were at stake if any follower of Jesus came anywhere near the tomb.

When the women at the tomb first saw Jesus, they clung to his feet. Given Jesus' response, they have may done this in part to make sure he wasn't going anywhere! However, Jesus told them that it was okay, he wasn't leaving yet, and to go tell the disciples to meet him in Galilee, about 63 miles to the north.

Why might reasonable people believe Jesus literally rose from the dead? Why might reasonable people doubt that happened?

GROWING

Where do you find yourself in this question of belief? Do you believe Jesus rose from the dead, or is there another explanation you believe explains Jesus' missing body?

Journal your thoughts here.

How do you respond to people who are not sure that the resurrection of Christ actually happened?

Write your thoughts here.

Throughout this quarter we've been asking the question, Why is Jesus so radical? What was radical about Jesus being dead, and then being alive again three days later? In what sense does the Resurrection validate the truthfulness of everything Jesus ever said or did?

Capture your reflections here.

PARTICIPANT GUIDE

LESSON 13: HOW CAN I KNOW JESUS IS REALLY ALIVE TODAY?

GREETING

Which one of your senses—sight, taste, touch, hearing, or smell—do you think you rely on most? If you had to lose one sense, which one would you choose to lose? (And if you've ever lost a sense, you're invited to share about that!)

BEHIND THE SCENES

The proofs of the physicality of Jesus' glorified body—that it had substance, could be touched, and could enjoy and consume food—turned out to be a big deal. During the early years of the church's existence, many false teachers crept in and tried to persuade the believers that Jesus was never a true human being—that he only appeared to be a man.

Nothing could be further from the truth.

Years after the Resurrection, when the apostles were combating these false ideas, they would have remembered how Jesus invited them to touch his hands and feet to reassure them he wasn't a ghost. He even sat down and ate with them. By doing this, Jesus demonstrated that his resurrection was real and that he was, indeed, alive.

GROUNDING

God's Word: Luke 24:36-53

36 While they were still talking about this, Jesus himself stood among them and said to them, "Peace be with you."

37 They were startled and frightened, thinking they saw a ghost. 38 He said to them, "Why are you troubled, and why do doubts rise in your minds? 39 Look at my hands and my feet. It is I myself! Touch me and see; a ghost does not have flesh and bones, as you see I have."

40 When he had said this, he showed them his hands and feet. 41 And while they still did not believe it because of joy and amazement, he asked them, "Do you have anything here to eat?" 42 They gave him a piece of broiled fish, 43 and he took it and ate it in their presence. ▼

44 He said to them, "This is what I told you while I was still with you: Everything must be fulfilled that is written about me in the Law of Moses, the Prophets and the Psalms."

45 Then he opened their minds so they could understand the Scriptures. 46 He told them, "This is what is written: The Messiah will suffer and rise from the dead on the third day, 47 and repentance for the forgiveness of sins will be preached in his name to all nations, beginning at Jerusalem. 48 You are witnesses of these things. 49 I am going to send you what my Father has promised; but stay in the city until you have been clothed with power from on high."

50 When he had led them out to the vicinity of Bethany, he lifted up his hands and blessed them. 51 While he was blessing them, he left them and was taken up into heaven. 52 Then they worshiped him and returned to Jerusalem with great joy. 53 And they stayed continually at the temple, praising God."

What questions and thoughts come to mind when you read through this passage? Capture those thoughts here.

GRAPPLING

GOING DEEPER

Many times Christians will not express their doubts and questions because they do not feel like it's safe to do so—that perhaps they'll be seen as some sort of heretic. Resolving our doubts is a great way to strengthen faith, so give people all kind of room, grace, and mercy when they start asking questions about matters of faith that might be fully resolved in your own mind.

The disciples had ample evidence that Jesus had died...yet there he stood. In what ways did Jesus meet them where they were—emotionally, physically, spiritually, or in other ways?

Why do you think Jesus took the time to make this additional point even when he was standing right there in front of them? And does this have any implications for us all these years later?

INTERESTING THOUGHTS SPARKED
BY OTHERS IN MY GROUP:

BEHIND THE SCENES

Did you know there are more than 350 prophecies about the Messiah in the Old Testament—and that Jesus fulfilled every single one of them to the smallest detail?

Jesus made it a point here—and with the disciples on the road to Emmaus—to show that everything predicted about him in the Law and through the Prophets came true. The odds of this happening with one person are astronomical—but not for the One of whom the prophecies spoke.

Faith stories shared today that encouraged me...

BEHIND THE SCENES

Luke tells us that Jesus "opened their minds" so that they could understand the Scriptures. This is just a humble reminder that we would not be able to accurately comprehend a single word of the Bible if it were not for the work of the Holy Spirit in our hearts, enabling us to understand God's truth and how those truths apply to our lives.

GROWING

Why is Jesus so radical?

Try to answer this question in just one sentence.